LOVE ON THE BEACH

Sue Bunney

Pen Press

First published in Great Britain by Pen Press

All paper used in the printing of this book has been made from wood grown in managed, sustainable forests.

ISBN 978-1-78003-624-3

Printed and bound in the UK
Pen Press is an imprint of
Indepenpress Publishing Limited
25 Eastern Place
Brighton
BN2 1GJ

A catalogue record of this book is available from
the British Library

Cover design by Jacqueline Abromeit

Cover image *Gorran Haven*, by Peggy Wright

Dedicated to Rob,
without whom this book would never have been written.

ACKNOWLEDGEMENTS

Many thanks to Vicky for giving me access to the lap top.

Special thanks to Michael, for his patience and good humour, with my efforts getting to grips with this new fangled machine.

Thanks to Amelia, Imi and Abi for their unwitting help in keeping me busy and grounded.

Thank you to Grace at Indepenpress.

Finally, a big thank you to the star of the book, the beautiful county of Cornwall, there is nowhere like it.

Sea Fever

I must go down to the seas again, for the call of the
    running tide
Is a wild call and a clear call that may not be denied.

I must go down to the seas again, to the lonely sea and
    the sky,
And all I ask is a tall ship and a star to steer her by.

John Masefield

CHURCH PARK

THE PERFECT CORNISH PASTY

or THE WAY TO A MAN'S HEART

(Just remember anyone can do it,
all you need is the right ingredients.)

RECIPE *(for two man-sized pasties)*

One pack of puff pastry
6ozs of beef skirt
Two medium potatoes
One medium onion
Half a small turnip
Seasoning
One beaten egg

METHOD

1. Cut the meat into small pieces.

2. Peel the onion and the potatoes and turnip and put into a bowl of water.

3. Divide the pastry in half and place on a floured board.

4. Shape each half into a circle and roll out. (Use a round dinner plate for size.)

5. Now chop the potato, turnip and onions into small pieces.

6. Place the vegetables into the middle of the pastry, (be sure to leave enough room around the pastry to gather it all together and seal).

7. Now on top of the pile of vegetables place the chopped meat, and a slice of butter. The butter will add flavour and yummy juices.

8. Add salt and pepper and brush the edges of the pastry circle with a little beaten egg…

9. Pull the edges of the pastry together and press together to seal.

10. Starting at the corner, roll the pastry edges over and under to crimp. Make the other pasty, (crimping should be easier the second time – it will come, I promise).

11. Brush with beaten egg and place on a greased baking tin. Make a small hole in the top of the pasty for the steam to escape.

12. Put both pasties into the middle of the oven at 180°C, 350°F, Gas Mark 5, for 40/45 minutes. (Remember, a fan oven is always hotter.) You can cover the pasties with greaseproof once the pastry is brown.

You can check if the filling is cooked by inserting a sharp knife through the breathing hole in the top of the pasty.

P.S. Cover with tin foil if the pastry is getting too brown!

CHAPTER ONE

Mackerel for Breakfast

It was one of those magical Cornish mornings, the tip of the sun glowing on the horizon, a hush lying over the cove and the promise of a perfect summer day about to begin. The tiny cove of Portmellon was still asleep, the curtains of the holiday cottages tightly closed. Inside the thick granite walls the summer visitors lay wrapped in their holiday dreams.

Silently we paddled out to our small boat, gently rocking at her mooring. We climbed aboard and Rob eased the oars into the rowlocks and began to row out towards Chapel Point, it seemed mean to attempt to start our temperamental old Seagull outboard while still in the cove. I sat in the stern, basking in the increasing warmth of the sun and gazing at the eccentric group of three whitewashed houses which stood clustered on the jagged headland reaching out into the sea. Chapel Point truly lived up to its name, the turrets and imposing architecture more suitable for a cliff top in Italy than perched on a rocky Cornish headland. The houses fascinated me, they stood out against the blue sea, a totally unexpected sight, nothing could have been more in contrast to the solid granite fishermen's cottages of Mevagissey across the bay.

A sleepy gull swooped down to check us out, landing gracefully on the sea beside us, he bobbed about, waiting to see if a free meal would be coming his way. It seemed as if we were the only people in the world awake, but I knew that the fishing boats from Mevagissey would have beaten us and would already be steaming out to the fishing grounds.

'Do you fancy some mackerel for breakfast?' Rob had asked, and with the lure of freshly caught fried mackerel he had me hooked. Our old Seagull engine started on the third pull, and we cruised out into the bay. We caught twelve silver mackerel, then turned back towards Chapel Point where our one crab-pot marker lay on top of the water. Rob turned off the engine and leant over to start pulling up the pot; there was always a delicious sense of anticipation when hauling the pot, a bit like finding buried treasure, you never knew what you would find. I watched fascinated then he suddenly dropped the dripping rope back into the water with an almighty splash.

'Quick row,' he yelled, and noting the rising panic in his voice I grabbed the oars.

'What's the matter?' I shouted, frantically trying to get the oars into the rowlocks.

'Look behind you!' he bawled. I turned around to scan the wide expanse of sea behind us, and was confronted by an ominous sight. A huge black fin was steadily weaving its way towards our tiny boat, and as it came closer I could clearly make out the unmistakable shape of a large grey shark. My heart pounding, I attempted to row, causing a great deal of splashing but not making much headway. Rob was attempting to start the engine which was always reluctant to start under normal conditions and clearly it wasn't going to change the habit of a lifetime. It gave a few weak splutters and died while I carried on rowing for England. When I could almost hear the crunch of huge teeth upon our clinker hull, the engine suddenly burst into life and we sped away from Cornwall's answer to *Jaws*, and back into the sanctuary of Portmellon cove.

'What's a shark doing in that close?' I shouted above the din of the engine.

'Don't know, it's only a basking shark, no teeth.'

'Then why the big panic?'

'It could have rubbed against the side and capsized us,' was his answer, but I noticed that he looked rather sheepish.

'Anyway, better to be safe than sorry,' he added and having regained his original tough Cornishman image, he began to stow away the fishing lines.

What am I doing here, I asked myself, at the crack of dawn, bobbing about in a tiny boat, in the depths of Cornwall with a Celtic version of Davy Crockett. I guess that I already knew the answer in spite of the shark, and various other setbacks along the way, which were bound to occur between a true countryman, like Robert and a townie like myself. They say that opposites attract, well you couldn't find two more opposite than us. Rob is a true Cornishman, utterly convinced of the fact that Cornwall has no equal anywhere else in the world and until I appeared on the scene, and shattered his idyllic existence, his life consisted of the local cricket club, snooker, fishing and work, in that order.

Then I arrived, escaping from a failed marriage, small son in tow, and everything changed, except the cricket and the fishing, hence the boat and the shark.

My grandfather had been a Mevagissey fisherman, so for me coming to Cornwall was a way of rediscovering my roots and finding that I fitted into the lifestyle almost as if I had been born to it. The slower pace of life and the different priorities, plus the stunning scenery, were just what I had been waiting for; add to all that my own Davy Crockett, life was complete.

We cruised into Portmellon and I gazed up to the top of the hill where I could see Church Park sitting solidly among the trees, the centuries-old farmhouse which was now our home.

The noise of the outboard faded away as we reached the beach, and the ancient clinker boat gently nosed her way onto the soft sand. I jumped out of the boat and stood barefoot in the waves which were idly lapping upon the beach. The primitive call of my ancestors, and the ageless echoes of the sea, combined to weave a subtle Celtic spell from which I knew there would be no escape.

As we made our way back up the hill towards Church Park and turned into the lane at the top I was reminded of the first time I had seen it.

'Let me show you where I have always wanted to live,' Rob had said, and without more ado had promptly loaded me up in the transport box, behind the tractor. I had to hang on for grim death, nearly falling out when we stopped in front of a gate leading into a very muddy lane. Hanging over the gate were the brown steaming heads of twenty large bullocks. Rob jumped off the tractor shouting at the great beasts as he opened the gate. We roared up the lane lurching from side to side, finally reaching the top to find an old stone and cob farmhouse which was surrounded by a walled garden.

'This is it,' Rob said, and my heart sank.

The poor old house was a sad sight. The roof was hanging by a thread, the empty windows stared forlornly out into the tangled mass of what once had been a garden.

'We'll need a machete to get through,' I said, but it was lost on Rob who was already beating his way through the undergrowth, determination proving better than any machete. I followed, pushing back the arms of a pale pink rose which was still vainly clinging to the old garden wall and flowering in spite of it. We reached the front porch and Rob inserted an old key into the rusty lock. It was a stable door, split into two parts; finally the top half yielded, and we were standing in the hallway. The creeping musty odour of neglect and decay oozed around us. Rob picked his way over the rotting floorboards, the kitchen was right in front of the main door, the dining room, to the right, led through to the sitting room. There were no passages, there was also no ceiling, and we could look straight up to the roof struts.

'How old is it?' I asked.

'Oh sixteenth or seventeenth century,' he airily replied.

What's a few centuries between friends, I thought but said nothing, I didn't want to dent his obvious enthusiasm.

'Built like a battle ship,' he continued.

'Looks like it's been in one,' I muttered under my breath, as I picked my way over the broken glass and fallen masonry.

'Just look at the thickness of those walls,' he commanded, pointing towards the windows, which I had to admit were set in a stone wall at least two feet thick. 'And, just look at that view.'

I peered through the broken window pane and realised that the old house did command a breathtaking view towards the white houses on Chapel Point.

'What do you think?' Rob asked.

'Well it's certainly in a great position,' I said and began to make my escape over the rotting floor boards.

We fought our way out through the garden, and at the gate I turned to look again at Rob's dream home. The light was fading, the old house looked desolate and sad, the empty windows staring accusingly back at me, as though condemning me for my negative thoughts.

'Great, wasn't it,' Rob observed, as he tied up the garden gate with old string.

'It's going to take a miracle to make it liveable,' I ventured, yet in that last glance, Church Park had suddenly become a possibility.

I was to learn that miracles do happen. Ours came in the form of a rosy-cheeked builder – he was local, he knew the house and he loved his job, a wonderful combination. Rob helped with the renovation, which seemed only fair, as he was fulfilling his dream to live in the old house.

Everyone was fascinated as the work got underway, and the layers peeled away to reveal the history of the place. An old clome oven was revealed in a corner of the kitchen. When they began to strip off the remaining roof they found centuries-old wooden pegs, which confirmed our suspicion that the house had originally been thatched. The roof trusses were simply thick branches of trees, which had been split in half and laid to hold the thatch. Rob became even more enthusiastic as they made each discovery. Though the front of the house was stone we discovered that the back was cob, a mixture of mud and straw, and which again dated the house way back into the early sixteenth century. As they began to dig out the old floors they found beach cobbles and old stone drains under the sitting room, which meant that the house went way back to the days when the farmer lived in one part of the house and his cattle lived in the other part, providing warmth for the whole building.

By this time, as each new piece of evidence was being unearthed, I began to understand why Rob was so enthusiastic about the place. It was a piece of history, which hopefully was being brought back to life. The new roof was a slate one, the windows were all replaced, a damp course was installed, the walls were replastered, and pale blue Rayburn cooker was given pride of place in the kitchen. Gradually the original character of the house began to emerge again and it was pulled and pummelled into the twentieth century.

News of what was happening spread through Mevagissey. Various people stopped me, with their individual stories of the old house on the hill. It was amazing, the different families who had memories of the place, generally through grandparents, or even great grandparents. I learnt that the house had been divided into two dwellings for one period, then reverted back to one, but that when the old couple who had rented it from the main farm had left, the place stayed empty for quite a few years. Now it was coming back to life; as people talked about the place, I realised that it was a piece of village history, and that we were so lucky to be a small part of it.

CHAPTER TWO

Calamity Sue

Church Park was ready to become a home again, all it needed was some furniture, but furniture cost money which was in short supply – I had come out of my marriage with nothing, and Rob had spent his single years having fun, saving money had not been his priority. Then when we heard that Heligan House, the old manor near Mevagissey, was selling up it seemed to be the answer to our problems. We wandered through the old house managing to acquire some great bargains. The rooms were huge, we got a beautiful top-quality carpet from one room which covered our sitting room and two bedrooms. We were delighted, then we made our way out into the tangled garden which surrounded the house – little did we know then that twenty years later Heligan gardens would become one of the biggest garden restorations in the country.

Church Park was complete, everything was ready, we got married on Rob's birthday.

'You are the best birthday present I have ever had,' he gallantly informed me. I was touched, but it made me feel as though I should have come gift-wrapped with a huge bow in a strategic place.

We went to Devon for a few days' honeymoon, Rob couldn't get more time off from the farm. It was an unusual honeymoon – we took my six-year-old son with us; friends obviously thought that we were mad to take him, but the truth of the matter was that he had been a big part of our relationship from the beginning, so to leave him at home was not an option. And I would never have considered getting married again unless I felt Christopher was happy with the situation. He was in his element and provided the other guests with great entertainment by announcing in a loud voice, 'We are having a honeymoon!'

Rob liked Devon, but would insist on comparing it to Cornwall. I was to learn that he would do this wherever we would go for the rest of our lives, his stock phrase being, 'It's very nice, but not as good as Cornwall.' Over the years we have been to many places and some have even gained 'almost as good as Cornwall'. I realised that Cornish pride of place is extremely strong.

School broke up for the summer and so we did what everyone at Gorran school did, we headed for the beach at Gorran Haven. Christopher was happy to see all his friends, they all learnt to swim, the mums spent time catching up on the local news, and the long summer days sped gloriously by.

Then suddenly the days began to get shorter, people began talking about school uniform, and autumn was upon us. We still went to the beach after school, but we realised that our beach days were numbered. Driving Christopher over to school at Gorran, I noticed that the sea had lost its bright blue and the waves which rolled in at Portmellon began to look darker and more menacing, splashing up onto the road. Then it began to rain, and the lane up to Church Park became muddy, the east wind roared in from the sea and winter caught us in its grip.

One evening Rob was over at Gorran playing snooker; he had piled logs on the fire and I had settled down to a quiet evening. Christopher was staying at friends for the night. The wind had been blowing relentlessly for days, bending the thorn trees which lined our lane almost in half, and whistling its way up towards the house, where it howled around the thick stone walls, wailing to be let in.

I had been in the kitchen making myself a cup of coffee and was walking back to the sitting room when the old stable door at the front of the house rattled loudly. There was an ominous crash outside. I stopped in my tracks.

'Who is it? Who's there?' I shouted, but there was no answer.

The door rattled again, I was in two minds – did I open it or run for the sitting room? I ran for the sitting room, and my imagination took off. What could I do? We were at the top of the hill at the end of a long lane, we didn't have a phone, Rob would not be back for ages, action was called for.

My eyes lit upon Rob's shotgun hanging on the wall. He had two guns, but as his shooting days were over, we decided to hang them on the wall as they fitted in with the style of the old house. I'm not going without a fight, I thought, and quickly unhitched the gun. Never one for half measures I hunted around for some cartridges. I had not the faintest idea of how to load, or shoot a gun, but based my actions upon all the western films I had seen. Also I had been the proud possessor of a pop gun as a child, I found that the shotgun worked on much the same principle. I broke open the gun, and slid the cartridges into the barrel. It all worked very well.

I sat on the settee feeling a whole lot better, my trusty gun upon my lap, I was ready for action. Calamity Jane had nothing on me.

Rob meanwhile, having enjoyed a quiet game of snooker, arrived back at the ranch to find Calamity Sue, gun cocked, ready to take on the entire Sioux nation single-handed.

Ashen-faced he retrieved the lethal weapon and delivered a stern lecture on the dangers of greenhorns and guns. He couldn't believe that I had managed to load the gun without having a clue as to what I was doing.

'Don't you ever do that again,' he said, 'you could kill someone.' The fact that his hand was shaking, as he took the gun from me, actually had more effect than what he said. I realised that I had gone a bit over the top, but if you have a vivid imagination, and are suddenly out in the wilds, then I figured a woman must do what a woman must do.

Later Rob began to take quite a bit of pleasure in recounting the episode to all our friends. Unfortunately the story got back to our local bobby, Hue, who didn't see the funny side of it. We received a visit from him, with the news that we were not allowed to keep a working gun hanging on a wall, and as Rob's licence for shooting had applied to when he was living at his father's farm, we were breaking the law.

'We only wanted it for decoration,' we told him.

'Then you will have to have the firing mechanism taken out,' he informed us.

We thought about the situation, and decided to give one of the guns to Rob's brother, back at home, and hand the other gun into the police station to avoid any more hassle. Rob would not be shooting any more.

Because Rob was busy hay making it was decided that I would hand the gun into the police station. When I saw the terrified expressions on people's faces as I marched through St Austell with the offending gun under my arm, I realised that I should have concealed it in a large bag. The jolly policeman behind the desk gratefully relieved the offending weapon, I think that he could see that he was dealing with a real greenhorn.

CHAPTER THREE

Down The Wood Pile

We did not have central heating at Church Park. The pale blue Rayburn in the kitchen was brilliant for providing a warm, cosy, heart of the house, but the large sitting room was heated by a wood fire. This was lit in an enormous fireplace, which the builder had created in a mad moment, and which could easily devour half a tree in an evening.

'We can have all the wood we want from the farm,' Rob informed me, 'it goes with the job.'

What he failed to say was that there was the tiny job of felling a tree, then cutting said tree into logs. Initially he set to work with great enthusiasm, creating a wood pile half way down our lane. Our first fire was quite an occasion; the sitting room was furnished and ready to use, all we needed was a roaring fire to complete the rural scene.

Rob took over the fire-lighting ceremony, and was gobsmacked when, after a few flickers, the tiny flames went out.

'Let me have a go,' I said, keen to succeed. 'You need more paper,' I added tactlessly. 'What's the idea of a wigwam?'

Rob was getting stressed, 'I always do it this way,' he answered, 'it's the only way to light a fire.'

I subsided and watched his second attempt. This included lying on his stomach, blowing into the smouldering sticks and paper, followed by putting an entire page of the *Cornish Guardian* over the front of the fireplace 'to draw it'. The entire procedure seemed to be taking rather a long time. I thought about suggesting getting some fire lighters, but because we were in the happy thrall of the newly married. I refrained from any more comments, and waited patiently for the flames to become the roaring log fire I had been promised.

Finally, when the ice was beginning to form, the flames did leap into life, so much so that we began to worry about the ability of the chimney to cope with the sudden heat after years of neglect. Cope it did, and we revelled in the magic of a real log fire. The smell of burning wood is unique, stirring the senses and appealing to the basic primitive human desire for warmth. I am quite convinced that the smell of a wood fire evokes memories of our ancestors handed down through the years and ingrained in our genes.

I did try telling Rob how I felt, but he wasn't a bit impressed by my flights of fancy. All he knew was that he was chopping wood for England, and that I was burning it like there was no tomorrow. We got to the situation when I would wait for him to go to the loo, and sneak a few logs on the fire, quickly rearranging the log basket to look as though no one had touched it. Rob manfully chopped wood, spending every evening after work, down at the wood pile. Not only did he chop his own wood, he actually felled the chosen tree himself, then transported it back to the wood pile. Wood fires, we quickly found out, burn at an amazing speed, and as the fireplace was so large, it gobbled up the logs with an endless appetite. The log basket never seemed to stay full for long.

'What are you doing with it?' became a familiar cry from my woodsman. He made it sound as though I was piling the logs on just to spite him.

'We have to keep warm,' I would answer, through gritted teeth.

Then, one Saturday, while he was on a wood cutting expedition, he cut down a tree which unfortunately fell down the wrong way, landing right on top of him, pinning him to the ground. Luckily, there was a slight hollow in the ground, where Rob was trapped, and after the initial shock he was able to wriggle out, and lived to fight another day. Cut and bruised, he made his way back home, and took great pleasure in recounting the story of his near brush with death, every time I so much as looked at a fresh log.

We continued to argue over the best way to light a fire, Rob still a firm believer in the old wigwam approach; me, an advocate of the good old fire lighter. Fire lighters were, to Rob, an admission of failure – he hadn't been brought up on such newfangled inventions, and he wasn't having them in his fire, no way. His parents were tenant farmers, life had been hard, and fire lighters were a luxury we couldn't afford, or so he thought. The result of this situation meant that when it was my turn to light the fire, I would make sure that he was still at work, and use two sometimes even three to produce a roaring fire for my master's return.

'Did you build a wigwam?' he would ask, eyeing the roaring flames with suspicion.

'I always do,' I would dutifully reply, which was quite true, but what I omitted to say was my wigwam always had at least two lovely efficient fire lighters slap bang in the middle.

Later on I ended up running the local cub group, and we would spend many happy hours in the woods, building fires and cooking sausages. Rob would often accompany us on these expeditions and would drive me mad, insisting on trying to teach the cubs to light wet wood and damp paper, doing his 'I'm building a wigwam', routine, while thirty cub scouts would be running wild, waiting for the odd flame to burn their sausages on.

I'm afraid that fire lighting was, and still is, one of those situations where we are both utterly convinced that we know best. Occasionally, I would be driven to wonder whether not being allowed to use fire lighters would be considered grounds for divorce. We were never a 'let's agree to differ' kind of couple – tempers would flare, unlike the fires, and even though we now have central heating, we can still manage to fight over the best way to light a fire on the beach or a barbecue.

CHAPTER FOUR

Refugee From The Farm

Gorran men are cricketers, Mevagissey men are footballers, both villages have achieved amazing success in their chosen games over the years, the two communities taking tremendous pride in the various cups which had been brought home. While we were courting, (for want of another suitable word) I have to admit I viewed cricket as a hobby, a pleasant way to pass a sunny afternoon. This just goes to show how naive I was. It was not until after our marriage that it finally dawned on me how vitally important cricket is to all cricketers, and especially to mine.

The first rainy Saturday reduced Rob to a picture of deepest despair. His cricket bag was packed, he bristled with eager anticipation, then disaster struck – it started to rain. There was no let-up, it continued to pour down, as only Cornish rain can – warm but wet, very wet. Rob paced up and down, like a caged lion, pausing only to gaze out of the window every two or three minutes, searching for a glimpse of blue sky.

'Is there enough to make a sailor a pair of trousers?' I asked, in an attempt to lighten the situation. There was no answer, 'surely you can rearrange the match, can't you?'

His face creased with pain at my gross insensitivity. It was obvious that his new wife had no idea of the sheer tragedy of the situation. I was to quickly learn that for Rob, cricket was a passion.

'It's what I live for,' he said, 'and you of course,' he added as an afterthought.

We could so easily have come to blows that first rainy Saturday, but the sight of a bedraggled figure, slowing plodding up our lane, luckily distracted us.

'It's Bess, said Rob, and we watched in silence as the old farm dog squelched her way up onto our lawn and collapsed in a sodden heap.

She was the farm dog at Bodrugan, where Rob worked, half a mile away. I had tried, on various occasions, to make friends with her but she would have none of it, curling her lip and sliding under the tractor. She obviously had a special relationship with Rob, had followed the tractor, and had worked out where he was now living.

I loved dogs, had never been allowed to have one, and I found it very hard to accept that here was a dog who resisted all my attempts at friendship.

'It's because she was born in the wild,' Rob would explain, and then went on to tell me the story of Bess's birth. It seemed that her mother, Nell, had given birth to various litters over the years; and, back then, the solution to unwanted pups on the farm had been to drown them at birth. Nell finally realised that if she stayed around the farm, she would lose her puppies, so she left the only security she knew, and made her way down the valley towards the sea. There, under a clump of sycamore trees, she found a disused badgers' hole, and this was the place she chose for her last litter of pups to be born in. I never tired of hearing the story, it confirmed what I had always believed, that animals have an intelligence which we cannot begin to comprehend.

Back at the farm, Nell's absence had been noted; Rob especially was concerned. They had a strong working relationship, and he was the only one who seemed to get close to her. A few days later she was spotted slinking back into the farmyard, looking for food, but she never stayed. Finally Rob managed to follow her back down the valley.

He found her guarding her snarling snapping brood of puppies who dashed down back into their den as he approached. The puppies, though wild, were beautiful, very fluffy and bright. By this time, of course, they were too old to be drowned. Nell had won her fight to keep her last little family, and they were left alone. Food was put out for her, and gradually she realised that they were all safe.

A few weeks later she amazed everyone by appearing in the farmyard, with the five puppies staggering behind her. Proudly she led them into the old mill house, where she slept and bedded them down in the hay. Homes were found for all the pups with various farmers in the parish, yet they remained wary of people for the rest of their lives. It was as though their mother had instilled into them that some humans have no respect for animals, and that they must always be on their guard.

Bess still lay in the, by now, heavily pouring rain. 'She won't come in, she never goes in at Bodrugan,' Rob informed me.

I tried to ignore the rain, and the half wild black dog curled up in a tight ball in the middle of the lawn. Finally, I could stand it no longer.

'I'm going to try,' I said, and headed for the kitchen and some custard cream biscuits. I opened the front door, and we stared at one another. I held out a biscuit, she gazed back steadily, never moving a muscle, her brown eyes following my every move.

'Come on, girl, look how wet you are,' I made my way towards her, talking the whole time. Then I stopped, within a few feet of her, and deposited a custard cream on the ground. I stepped back and put down another one; without looking at her I proceeded to lay a trail of biscuits up to our door and into the hall, leaving the door open. I left her to it and went into the sitting room to watch out of the window.

Bess stayed exactly where she was, the minutes ticked by, Rob heaved a sigh. 'I told you she wouldn't come in,' he said yet again.

'Oh well, it was worth a try,' I answered, not willing to let him have been proved right. I glanced out again and could hardly believe my eyes, Bess had slowly got to her feet. I held my breath – what was she going to do? Would she turn tail and plod back to the farm, had she had enough of this meddling woman?

She stood, it was clear that she was uncertain about what to do next, I could almost read her thoughts, then, after what seemed ages, she gingerly walked towards the first biscuit, put her head down and sniffed it. We held our breath, she looked up at the window – she knew that we were watching. After what seemed like an age, she picked it up and ate it. Would she like the taste? Farm dogs are not in the habit of getting custard creams, but she seemed to be developing a taste. Walking to the next one, she picked it up and then followed the biscuit trail until she finally stood, dripping wet, in our tiny hall.

She was terribly nervous, but I like to think that she had finally realised that I was not an enemy, and that the biscuits were my way of offering a hand, or rather, a paw, of friendship; also, of course, she knew that Rob, the one person she really trusted, was inside at the end of the biscuit trail.

Rob came into the hall completely amazed at the turn of events, he knelt down beside her, talking to her all the time. I held back, frightened to break the spell. Then Rob got to his feet, she took one look at me and bolted up the stairs to the top landing, where she sat watching us.

'Leave her,' Rob said and went back to his rain watch.

I decided that having got that far with her I wasn't going to give up. I grabbed another handful of biscuits and inched my way up the stairs, gently talking to her, all the way. Stopping one step below her, I held out the last biscuit. She gave me a long look, then with an air of resignation she accepted it from my hand. It was a wonderful feeling, we were friends.

CHAPTER FIVE

Dog Called Bess

Give a dog a custard cream and you have a friend for life. Bess was taken back to the farm that evening, but I think the biscuits and the attention all proved to be very attractive to an old farm dog who was generally used to living out in the barn.

After that first visit I would often look out of the window to see her familiar black figure slowly plodding up the lane. She never barked to be let in, but would curl up on the lawn like a polite guest, waiting to he asked inside. Very often Rob would arrive home, chugging up the lane on his tractor, and within ten minutes later Bess would arrive as well. In the beginning Rob insisted on taking her back, but she still kept coming, and eventually I persuaded him to let her spend the night, knowing that she had to go back to work the next morning.

By now we had acquired a dog of our own, a black long-legged mongrel puppy we called Bambi, and it was very touching to see Bambi's delight at greeting Bess and to watch the two of them playing. With maternal humour, Bess put up with Bambi jumping all over her, chewing her ears, and indulging in numerous mock battles. When it was meal time I would call Bambi inside and Bess would follow on, slowly, and always a little apprehensive.

Feeding Bambi, it seemed mean not to offer Bess a small supper, and then to see them both curled up together by the fire, completed the picture of doggy bliss. The problem was, that the next morning Bess had to go to work, and that meant chasing after the tractor down into

Portmellon and then climbing Bodrugan hill which was very steep. After all this she then had to put in a day's work on the farm, herding sheep and bullocks.

I have to admit I nagged, no other word for it.

'Can't you carry her on the tractor?'

'Nowhere to put her,' came the answer.

'She's not a young dog, there must be something you can do.'

'Poor Bess,' I would say in the evenings, 'you can see she is worn out.'

'She's tough, she's a farm dog.'

'So farm dogs don't get tired? She could have a heart attack trying to keep up with you on the tractor.'

I kept going until finally, to shut me up, Rob got out his tool kit and constructed a wooden seat behind his. The first morning he lifted Bess into it and Christopher and I watched nervously. Would she like it? She had never been in anything like it before – would she try to jump out?

We needn't have worried, she sat there like a queen, her brown eyes shining, and looking at her face that day I wouldn't have been surprised to see her wave a paw goodbye. This situation continued for a few years, but eventually after being carried to work, she would decide that she had done enough and head for home, back to Church Park. This became embarrassing for us – Jeffery, the farmer, would have to come looking for his dog if Rob was out in one of the other fields working.

Finally it was agreed, Bess could officially retire, they would get a new farm dog. This seemed an ideal answer to the problem, but there was a hitch – Bess loved retirement, but every so often she would get bored and miss the farm. Then she would make her way back to see how they were getting on without her. Then one evening she decided to bring Panda, the new farm dog, back home with her.

I imagined the conversation.

'Cream biscuits, lovely food, warm bed, come with me.'

Panda was well named – very fluffy, black and white and very bouncy. She appeared at our door with Bess. She was delighted to see us, she had heard so much about us, she greeted me like a long-lost friend. Rob took one look at my face and was adamant – no biscuits, no pats, nothing, she had to go back immediately. He loaded her into the car and all we could see was a confused black and white face staring back at us, she couldn't understand what she had done wrong. She never arrived at Church Park again, but in later years she was to turn up on another doorstep, but we didn't know that then.

CHAPTER SIX

Me and Cricket

The Old Cricket Pavilion
(from a painting by D.F. Thomas)

Before I got married for the second time, if anyone mentioned the word 'cricket' I immediately thought of the beach version – dads and sons having a knock-around on the sand. Then I emigrated to Gorran, and still it hadn't dawned on me exactly what the word cricket actually meant to an ardent cricketer.

When Rob said he played cricket, I imagined it was just a hobby – how wrong I was. I was soon to discover that cricket is a passion, a reason for living, a constant source of conversation throughout the entire summer. Just to drive past the cricket field brings a smile to Rob's face. Saturdays, I was to learn, are devoted to cricket. Rainy Saturdays are a cause for deep despair; sunny Saturdays are the best thing in the world, happiness reigns.

The cricket field is situated at the top of the hill, at the head of Gorran village, directly opposite the school, made famous in Anne Treneer's book, *School House in the Wind*. The cricket field should have the same title, as the wind has played a dominant part in matches over the years. I've seen players being tossed around by powerful gusts, their whites flattened against their legs, their shirts billowing out behind them, their faces blue with the cold as they battled against the elements in those first matches of the season.

The view from Gorran cricket field is spectacular and makes up, in a large way, for the ridiculous amount of time we have all spent up there. When I say we, I mean, of course, cricket wives, who need to make a choice – 'if you can't beat 'em, join 'em'. The field looks down onto Gorran village, the solid grey tower of the church, fringed with trees, the cottages nestling in the valley. Away in the distance, across the fields, the towering white clay hills of St Austell, and to the right a glimpse of the sea and St Austell bay.

'Come and watch,' Rob suggested casually one evening, at the beginning of our relationship, and thinking it was a one-off situation, I agreed. It was a beautiful summer evening, the late rays of the day lying lazily on the green fields, the cricket field bathed in a warm golden glow. The cricketers looked angelic in their whites, there was the rhythmic sound of the ball against the bat, groups of spectators were arranged around the field – it was an idyllic scene.

'I'll park the car up in the right-hand corner,' my cricketer told me. At that particular stage in our relationship, it wasn't common knowledge that we were going out together, or so I thought. As I made my way along the boundary that evening, I could almost feel eleven pairs of eyes watching my every move. What I didn't realise at the time was that coming to watch Rob play cricket was a public declaration of commitment – we were an item. When you live in a small community your life becomes public property, everyone is interested in everyone else, so much so that they often seem to know what you are going to do, even before you actually do it. Gossip is part of life, news in Cornwall travels up and down the county – the jungle drums are alive and well down here.

'Any news?' we all say, and we don't really mean the government or the economic situation, we mean village news, anything on our own patch, much more interesting than boring, depressing old world news.

After this initial introduction to the cricket field, it seemed only a short step to watching the Saturday matches. These seemed to go on for ever, beginning at two and often still going strong at seven thirty. Still, it kept them all out of mischief, and though I didn't have a clue what it was all about, I began to appreciate the fact that it gave us all a reason to get together. Rob made sure that he asked me to the best away matches, visiting Lanhydrock and Boconnoc, both with marvellous grounds and wonderful parklands where the children could play to their hearts' content. We stalked deer at Boconnoc, spending hours in the grounds, delighted to suddenly come upon the herd grazing under a majestic copper beech. Christopher found a pair of discarded antlers among the bracken, and brought them back as a trophy. The cricket wives would all sit together and have their picnics, while the children got stuck up trees or played their own games of cricket at the side of the ground.

Gradually I became hooked, not on the game, which I still didn't understand at all, due mainly to the fact that numbers were involved, and though I grasped the fact that hitting the ball was the main thing, the rest of it made no sense at all. It was the social side of the game which appealed to me, and so, when I was casually invited to be on the tea rota, it was done in such a way that I almost felt honoured to be included in the ritual. How little I knew, at that innocent stage.

The pavilion, in those days, was a long, blue wooden hut, situated in the bottom corner of the field. There was no electricity, the water was heated by two gas cylinders, in a huge urn which balanced precariously on the top. The cricket teas were laid out on three long trestle tables, which were covered with red-and-white checked clothes. Gorran cricket club was proud of its teas, and once captured onto the tea rota I quickly realised why. There were hundreds of sandwiches to be made, all cut into dainty sizes, and with various fillings. Ladies on the tea rota were expected to bake a cake at home and bring, to add to the feast. Jam and cream splits needed to be prepared, plus all the other 'boughten cakes' which had to be cut up and placed on the pale blue china. At the same time as doing all this, we were expected to walk around the field and sell raffle tickets to all the spectators, provide drinks for the players, and minister to any injured cricketers along the way. And last, but not least, to keep an eye on our children, who might be climbing on the pavilion roof or attempting to start up the roller at the side of the pavilion. Once the tea was prepared we always heaved a sigh of relief, and so would the resident sparrows who lived nearby. They would then take it in turn to nip in through a hole in the roof and, while our backs were turned, would merrily hop up and down the table taking their pick of the cricket tea. Finally we had to cover it all with another of the huge check cloths. But when I was on teas I always kept a store of crumbs to put on one corner, I felt it was mean to deprive the birds of their afternoon tea.

My first cricket tea was a nerve-racking affair, I was told we had to count the number of overs left to be sure to have the tea made, ready to pour, when the hordes of hot sweaty cricketers descended upon us. The pavilion was small, the men were big, and had to file in to the bottom benches, then filling up the rest, all packed tightly together. The tea ladies would then pass the cups of steaming tea down along the tables. There would be a short silence, punctuated only by the odd comment and the slurping of tea as the teams fell upon the food. Then the worse bit would come when the men would require their cups refilled. This meant one of the tea ladies standing on sentry duty with the huge tea pot, a bit like Alice in Wonderland, waiting for the call, and then having to lean over the men and pour the required cup of tea. Any new lady on the tea run was fair game, and the whole situation made me fee! as though I was at the Mad Hatters Tea Party, in a harem.

Christopher became almost as obsessed with cricket as Robert, spending hours in the nets, playing with other cricketers' children, their matches often lasting even longer than the men's. That first year of cricket, 1972 was a magical year, Gorran seemed to win everything, The Roseland Evening League and the Eastern League Division One and then the Edwards Cup against Penzance, in a nail biting finish at Truro which we all watched with baited breath. All these wins meant much celebrating, retiring to the local pub, the Barley Sheaf, and we all got quite blasé as every cup was won and the obligatory photographs were taken. As it was my first introduction to the game, I assumed that this was what always happened; I was to realise later that 1972 was a special year, in more ways than one.

CHAPTER SEVEN
Cornish Cricket

Cornish cricket is divided into two leagues. We played in the Eastern League, the final would be against the Western League, or 'down west' as they were referred to, and there was always that carrot at the end of the season if we were lucky enough to get into the final. Although our Saturdays were dominated by cricket and would be for the next thirty years, I still didn't have a clue what it was all about, numbers having never been my strong point, however Rob cleverly initiated me into the attractive aspects of this obsession by selling the beauty of the different grounds, plus drinks at the end of the match, and offering fish and chips on the way home.

'You'll love Boconnoc,' he assured me.

'What's so special about it?' I asked.

'Wait and see,' was the reply.

You always need a sunny day for cricket, and we were lucky that day because the sun came slanting down through the trees as we made our way along a narrow winding lane leading to Boconnoc estate.

Rob stopped the car in front of a large wooden gate, 'Hop out,' he instructed, 'make sure you close it.'

We drove down through a magnificent wood of beech and oak trees, turning off along a track which led up to the cricket pitch sitting happily in the middle of the wood. An old cottage with a pitched roof stood beside the pavilion, there were coops of chicken clucking busily in the cottage garden. The cricket pavilion provided the next surprise – it was built entirely of logs, an original log cabin in the middle of a Cornish wood. There were no windows, just wooden shutters and inside were long tables and wooden benches, whoever had built the pavilion had obviously used the local resources to great effect.

The cottage reminded me of Hansel and Gretel, I half expected the wicked stepmother to appear, and all the log cabin needed was a horse tied up at the front. The mixture of styles was fascinating, add to that the herd of fallow deer who roamed the woods and who would suddenly appear on the pitch in the middle of the game. Forget 'rain stopped play' we had 'deer on pitch stopped play'.

Everyone would hold their breath as the deer nervously made their way onto the grass, stopping to nibble daintily, ears pricked, their soulful eyes watching for the slightest movement, ready to take off in a second. They never stayed for long, one would put its head up to the breeze and the telepathy would be instant, they would take flight, leaving us all wondering if we had been dreaming.

Then the children would be desperate to follow them, so leaving the men to continue with their game off we would go deer tracking. The problem was the deer were all of the Greta Garbo mould, they had to be alone, and having given us a taster they vanished back into the wood. It did not matter, they were there, all we had to do was find them again; but it was never that easy, they were elusive, but that made it all the more enthralling for the children – tracking the deer through the beautiful woods on a sunny afternoon was their idea of heaven. When Christopher found a discarded deer antler on one of these expeditions, you would have thought he had chanced on gold. Forget your computer games, all you need is a cricket pitch, a herd of deer, a Cornish wood, and a sunny afternoon.

Wadebridge was another favourite. 'Needle matches at Wadebridge,' Rob would mutter as we sped along towards the north coast. The cricket pitch was situated in the middle of a huge sports field with the river bordering the side of the pitch. When a batsman managed to hit a six, the ball would often sail high in the air, up over the bank landing with a splash into the fast-flowing river. A special net was provided for this eventuality, with the nearest fielder sprinting towards the bank, looking as though he had suddenly given up on cricket, and decided instead to go fishing – which in effect he had, but his catch was a cricket ball, not a fish, and if he was successful he was always greeted with a small cheer.

Wadebridge came a close second to Boconnoc because of the play park – parks were in short supply in our neck of the woods, the best one being at St Austell. The park at Wadebridge had a huge slide, and loads of roundabouts and to our kids it was the equivalent of Disneyland. Christopher and his friends would spend the entire afternoon in childhood heaven, only coming back to replenish their energy levels with huge amounts of food. This left the mums, other cricketing wives and followers to watch the cricket and catch up on any local gossip. I was beginning to get a small idea of what the game was all about, but I have to admit that the gossip still held my attention more than the cricket, though by now even I would stop chatting if one of our team took a mighty swipe at the ball sending it towards the river and the fishing net.

A Cornish childhood is unique, the beach playing a major role in the lives of Gorran children; very often the cricket pitches were only a stone's throw from the beach, giving us the chance to find and explore other beaches in the county. Bude, on the north coast, was situated on the very edge of the cliff, providing the players with a stunning view of the white-capped waves, though often very windy. 'Always blowing a gale at Bude,' Rob would say, 'you need to be anchored down.' We didn't care, we left them to it and headed for the beach, finding a huge natural swimming pool cut out of the rocks, spending the afternoon swimming, and then back to find out if we had won the match – in which case it would be stop on the way home for the entire team to celebrate, or long faces greeting us which meant hours of discussion on where it all went wrong, but we still got a drink, and possibly fish and chips on the way home, so life was pretty good.

All the cricket pitches had their different personalities, at Liskeard the fielders had to dice with death when the ball went into the garden of one of the bungalows nearby. The garden was patrolled by a huge black dog who waited, teeth bared, for the ball to land in his garden and for an unsuspecting fielder to hop over his hedge. Eventually after a few near misses, which resulted in players coming out like rockets, no one was allowed to retrieve the ball except the local policeman who luckily played for Bude and who carried the required clout.

Rob started playing cricket when he was ten years old; his father, a farmer, played for Gorran and Rob and his brother were introduced at an early age to the game. They would play in the road outside the farm, with a milk churn for a wicket. The obsession grew, many of the players were farmers, and after a week spent working alone for much of the time, the cricket field provided a welcome respite. Cars were in short supply, so the whole team would pile into two cars and head off into the wilds of Cornwall. At Ladock they would have to clear the cow pats off the pitch before the game could commence, and at Ruan Lanihorne Rob remembers a player being chased by an angry goose who lived at the bottom of the field. The players would often remember other clubs by the quality of their cricket teas, these would form a vital part of the entire proceedings, and still do, to this day. Jam and cream splits, piles of sandwiches, cakes, endless cups of tea, all served to twenty-two hungry, sweaty men, who devour the lot and then rush out to play the second innings. Healthy eating hasn't hit cricketing in Cornwall yet, not on a Saturday afternoon anyway.

CHAPTER EIGHT

Summer Visitors – or 'What Were They Called'

The tourist trade has always flourished in Cornwall, beginning with the few intrepid travellers who would undertake the endless journey from London and beyond in a fleet of cars laden with nannies, maids, and cooks, and ending up in some huge granite-built mansion perched on the cliffs, having a Cornish holiday. The Cornish tended to regard these early tourists as novelties, examples of another species, who bore no relation at all to the real things in life, such as mining, farming and fishing. They were tolerated, and unknowingly provided the locals with some welcome entertainment after the rigours of a hard winter. When asked a condescending question, by a plummy yacht owner, it became quite a competition to see who could give the most outrageous answer, in the broadest dialect, yet keeping a straight face. These same fishermen would spend hours sitting on the quay, discussing the political situation of the day. The value of their lifestyle was inherent, they knew exactly who they were, and if there was any condescending to be done, they were the ones doing it.

The Cornish have no respect for the upper classes, but what they do have respect for is the arts, due mainly to their Celtic forefathers. So, painters and writers, actors and those involved in the media, do command attention. Some years back, before the film industry descended on Cornwall, as it now has, a production company came to Mevagissey to make a film. The star of the film, was a Hollywood great – Clarke Gable. Clarke Gable was a friendly, hunting, fishing, sort of chap and as much of the filming was actually done on Mevagissey quay, he became a familiar sight to all the fishermen. The story in the film included a car chase along the outer quay, with the car going off the quay and into the water. This obviously required quite a bit of disruption in the everyday life of the fishermen, but they were most accommodating, and interested in the film-making technique. The entire company would drink in the pubs, and it was nothing to hear fishermen commenting, 'Me and Clarke Gable is having a drink tonight', or 'I was saying to Clarke, that stunt man, 'ee ain't got it right, 'ee wants ter stay under water fer longer, tisn't lookin' as good as it could.'

By the time we entered the tourist trade in the late sixties, bed and breakfast was an established industry. Church Park had four bedrooms, and we reasoned that the extra money would be very useful. Having been a Home Economics teacher, I felt confident to set up business. We began by acquiring some more beds, then extra cutlery and finally we were ready for business. Funds were stretched so we painted our own sign, and waited for our first customer.

We were not that easy to find, so I had added arrows and the odd bit of decoration to encourage the more adventurous visitor up our lane. They began to arrive. I think my hand-painted sign gave an indication that it was not your average hard-headed businesswoman at the helm. We provided huge breakfasts and threw in family entertainment for free. I went completely over the top to make our guests feel welcome, so much so that many of them never seemed to want to leave, and would still be sitting over their breakfast, at twelve, when Rob roared up the lane for his lunch.

The only way that I could cope with having complete strangers in the house was to treat them all as personal friends. All new arrivals would be shown their rooms and then offered a cup of tea in our large chintzy sitting room. Rob would arrive back from a day on the farm, often smelling of manure and looking decidedly rustic, which we found almost always seemed to appeal to visitors from the cities. They would inevitably begin by asking questions about the house and farm, at which point Rob would launch into a potted history of Church Park followed, quite often, by his own life story.

I think that for most visitors, the tea and chat gave them a feeling of belonging; also we got to know them, which had to be an advantage considering we were likely to meet while queuing for the bathroom. It helps to be reasonably friendly under these kind of circumstances. Now, of course, most bed and breakfasts are en suite, you never see your fellow guests, so miss out on the obligatory 'good morning' while clutching your sponge bag to your brand new dressing-gown.

Once we had done the 'tea and biscuits' hit, I would produce a front door key. 'You will want a key,' I would say to all and sundry, never mind that I had never set eyes on them, until half an hour ago; giving them a key meant that I was free to take Christopher to the beach after school, a treat I was not going to miss. It never occurred to me that anyone might take advantage of my actions, and no one ever did. People came back, year after year, often sitting in the old walled garden, if we were out, and greeting us like long lost, friends when we arrived back.

'Who are they?' we would hurriedly whisper to each other, while I was making the tea. 'Can you remember their name?' It didn't really matter, they remembered us, and knew all about us.

'How's the cricket going?'
'Bess is looking fatter.'
'Have you caught any crabs this year?'

Yes, they certainly remembered us, and obviously never thought for a moment that we could have possibly forgotten them.

Some we could never forget. One chap made an everlasting impression, when he booked in with an eighteen-year-old girl draped all over him.

'I bet that's not his wife,' I said to Rob.

Sure enough, when he sidled into the kitchen on the Sunday morning, and bold as brass asked if he could book a fortnight in August – for his wife and family – he added, 'Oh, by the way, that isn't my wife I'm with, but you probably guessed that, didn't you?'

'Umm... yes, well no... I mean... ahh, when did you say?' Trying to appear worldly and unshockable I solemnly took down his holiday booking, not daring to look at Rob's face, which was a picture.

Two honeymooners provided our most embarrassing moment. They understandably retired to bed early, unfortunately their bedroom was directly above the sitting room. We were doing our usual thing, having coffee and a chat with our other guests, when the chat suddenly stopped, as the ceiling above us began to shake and there was the unmistakable sounds of the bed springs beginning to twang. Realising what was happening I began to talk loudly, hoping to drown out the sound of the activity upstairs. This simply didn't work, I gave up. We all stopped pretending to ignore the rumpus which was going on above us, staring up towards the ceiling in undisguised admiration.

'That has to be a *Guinness Book of Records* job,' Rob remarked, as we all gave up trying to compete with the sound effects and made our way to bed. What was worrying me was the fact that our other, middle-aged, guests were in the bedroom next door to the record breakers. I considered offering Rob's ear muffs, which he wore in the tractor, but decided against it, after all they were all only paying one pound and ten shillings each a night, they would have to put up with the sound effects.

This incident was followed by another one concerning the teenage daughter of a family who had stayed with us the previous summer. She arrived, out of the blue, with two friends; I naturally made them all welcome and duly issued them with a key. They set off to discover the night life of Mevagissey, and we went to bed.

I was awoken from a deep sleep by Rob whispering loudly in my ear.

'Kate's back.'

'Good,' I muttered, and turned over.

'She isn't alone,' he bellowed in my ear.

Still the penny didn't drop, I wanted to get back to sleep, I didn't see why I should be treated to a running commentary on what was happening to our guests.

'She's brought a man back with her,' he finally yelled into my ear. I realised that I would have to wake up, we obviously had a minor crisis on our hands.

'I'm not having this, it could be anyone, what would her parents think?' Rob was bristling with righteous indignation, he was determined to defend Kate's honour. I had a feeling that he could be a bit late on that score, but I could see it was without doubt, a delicate situation.

'I'm turning him out,' Rob informed me.

'Right, good idea,' I said, and buried my head in the pillow.

'I'm going to do it now.'

'Fine,' I replied.

'Are you coming?'

'What?' I couldn't believe my ears. 'No way,' I said, by now wide awake.

'Right then, I'll go by myself,' he said, in between pacing up and down. Rob hates any kind of confrontation, anything for a quiet life.

I watched in breathless fascination as he reached the door and vanished onto the long landing outside. I waited for the wham bang of the interloper being flung down the stairs, it was like some Victorian melodrama.

What actually happened was the sound of some very embarrassed whispering, followed by some hurried footsteps along the landing. There was the sound of the front door being gently closed and footsteps going down the garden path.

'What happened?' I asked, as a much calmer and somewhat chastened Robert, slid into bed beside me.

'Well, I knocked on her door, and told her he had to leave. But when he got up, I realised that he was six foot, at least, and big with it.'

'Did he go?' I enquired.

'Oh yes, no problem,' said Rob.

Silently, I digested the information – Robert is five foot ten, on a good day. I realised that he could, so easily, have bitten off more than he could chew. I felt he needed a pat on the back, for effort and good intentions.

'Well done,' I said, 'you've probably saved her from a fate worse than death.' I smothered a rising giggle.

There was silence from old honourable beside me, then, 'I wouldn't have bothered, if I'd known he was going to be that size,' he confessed.

We both chuckled in the darkness, it was all part of life's rich tapestry, but we seemed to be getting more than our fair share.

CHAPTER NINE

Quack and Thumper

Our family continued to grow, with the appearance one sunny morning of a duck. We had been subjected to two days of strong east wind, and the sea down at Portmellon had been mountainous, washing up over the road and houses making it impossible to get across at high tide. Rob had gone off to work, only to return ten minutes later carrying a very sorry-looking duck.

I was in the middle of cooking the visitors' breakfasts, and the last thing I needed was an orphan duck.

'He was washed up at Portmellon,' he hastily informed me, 'I'll put him in this box, see you later.'

With that he was gone, leaving me with the duck who by now was feeling decidedly better and was quacking loudly. I carried on frying the eggs, accompanied by the sound of increasingly demanding quacks.

'We have a duck in the kitchen,' I informed my bemused looking city visitors, who were in no doubt as to the fact owing to the sounds now echoing loudly into the dining room. We called our duck 'Quack', and he lived in a hastily constructed run in the back garden. Rob dug out a small pond for him and he gradually regained his health. It became obvious that he was ready for his freedom and the wild open spaces, so we decided to put him in a larger pool, which had been part of an old well at the top of our lane, outside the front gate. We felt that here Quack would have the opportunity to fly off if he wanted to, but that also he would be able to stretch his wings. I fully envisaged a truly happy ending to our interlude with

Quack, and had a definite picture of his first flight to freedom, with us standing below as he took off into the blue.

What happened was that we went off for a short walk, leaving Quack in his pool. When we returned we were desolate to find no sign of our fathered friend, simply a scattering of soft downy feathers gently blowing in the breeze.

'What's happened to him?' Christopher asked sadly.

'Oh he's probably flown off to find some other ducks,' we said hopefully.

Secretly, we wondered if a passing dog had sealed his fate; we would never know, but I favoured the thought of his flight to freedom, imagining Quack, living down in the valley at Portmellon, surrounded by his own happy family of happy, healthy, ducklings – but then, I always have been a sucker for happy endings.

Though we lost Quack, we still had Thumper, a huge white rabbit of Christopher's. Thumper, unfortunately, had a problem – he had been Houdini, in another life, and was always escaping.

'I've just seen your rabbit in the lane,' our bread man would cheerfully inform me. I would have to drop whatever I was doing and spend the next hour chasing an extraordinarily agile rabbit up and down the lane. The bread man, whose name was Lionel, seemed to take a perverse pleasure in bringing the news of Thumper's escape.

This was in the days of bread and meat being delivered to your door, before freezers and supermarkets took over our lives and removed the social contact of the small shop and the bread and milk man. The fact that we were somewhat off the beaten track didn't deter Lionel – his van would chug up the lane twice a week, and there was always time for a chat. The news would vary, according to what titbits he had picked up on his way around. His personal life also would be included; his wife was having a baby, they wanted a boy, he was thinking about changing his job, they were planning a holiday in the Scilly Isles, we covered it all. I enjoyed these little chats except for one thing, the arrival of Lionel always seemed to act as a signal for Thumper to go walkabout.

This state of affairs continued, until one day Thumper vanished completely. We searched high and low and finally agreed that his continual bids for freedom had to be realised – there were obviously some very seductive rabbits in the fields behind Church Park, and it was only fair to let Thumper take his pick of what the world outside his pen could offer. Whenever I took the dogs for a long walk in the fields I was always on the look out for any brown and white rabbits. I had the distinct feeling that Thumper was a rabbit who would make the most of his new-found freedom.

CHAPTER TEN

Me and Baden Powell

When I first moved to Cornwall, Christopher and I lived with my parents in Gorran Haven. There wasn't a playgroup at that time, but a group of young mums got together and Gorran Playgroup was formed. Like so much in Cornwall, back in the late sixties and early seventies, it was a do-it-yourself playgroup which took off and grew rapidly.

Then I got married again, and moved to Church Park, near Mevagissey, and we had to decide which school Christopher would go to – Mevagissey or Gorran. Because he had made so many friends at playgroup, and because we had spent so many summer days on the beach at Gorran Haven, Gorran school was our choice. No more playgroup duties I thought, then after two years he arrived home from school one day with the news that he wanted to join cubs.

'That's a great idea,' I said, in all innocence. The cub pack was based at Gorran, and I happily drove him over the following week to get him enrolled. While chatting to the leader, I foolishly mentioned that I had been a teacher.

'That's marvellous,' the leader enthused. 'You could give us a hand if we were stuck.'

'I'm afraid I wasn't a Brownie,' I said quickly.

'That doesn't matter at all, you'd be great,' came back the reply.

Like cricket teas, the entire situation had been handled with such ease that, without knowing quite how it happened, within two months I was Akela, and running the show. Skip, meanwhile had vanished into the sunset taking early retirement. 'This really isn't me,' I kept saying to anyone who would listen, but nobody wanted to know. Somehow I was swept along by the sight of twenty eager shining little faces, also I was naive enough to believe that someone else would come along who was ideally more suited to the situation – after all, I had taught Home Economics to girls, a cub pack was a totally different ball game.

Thrown in at the deep end, I discovered that cubs are like a time-bomb waiting to go off – their energy levels are amazing. Full of life and vigour, a cub requires constant action to keep him happy – I found, to my cost, that being shut in the church rooms with an entire cub pack required the constitution of an ox. 'Keep 'em busy' became my motto; we did it all starting with the arrow badges. These badges were a godsend – they cleaned their shoes, getting polish on everything but the shoes; I produced a camp bed and they learnt to make it like a real one (no duvets in those days, blankets and sheets kept them busy). They were supposed to bring a note from home saying that they had made their bed, for a week. One mother actually rang me up to say that her little boy was having nightmares, getting wound up in the sheets, and could I please stop this bed-making lark, because she was fed up with having to extricate her son from his bedclothes every night. Continuing on the domestic front, all the cubs learnt to make a pot of tea, with me standing behind them praying that their weedy little arms could actually lift the teapot.

Story telling was one way of keeping them quiet. I got Rob to construct a camp fire which glowed, and I would sit the little dears around it, turn off the lights and tell stories.

'Tell us a ghost story, Akela!' they would yell, and always one to weave a yarn I would oblige. The trouble was that with the only light the glimmer of the fire, and the wind whistling around Gorran Church rooms, the temptation to elaborate on the ghost theme proved too much for me. Also the fact that little monsters could be reduced to absolute silence by a really scary ghost story, seemed to be the answer to a cub leader's prayer. When I got two telephone calls from parents saying their little darlings were coming back from cubs afraid to go to sleep, I decided that my ghost stories had possibly been a little too effective.

When we had exhausted all the domestic tasks, I decided to rope Robert in, to make kites. This was one of his many practical skills; he and Christopher would spend hours flying home-made kites in the fields behind Church Park. I reckoned that actually making the kites would keep the entire pack busy for at least two evenings and then, hopefully, as spring was coming we could have an evening flying the kites in Gorran school field.

Robert, fired with enthusiasm, suddenly decided to use dowel rods instead of his usual bamboo. I think he thought that dowel rods would look better. The cubs loved the making process, they cut and glued to their hearts' content, and then the great day arrived. We marched them up to the field. There was a good breeze blowing – perched on top of the hill, Gorran school is notorious for strong winds – it was ideal. The cubs gathered in the field, a mass of happy shining faces, they were all on their best behaviour. I began to feel really happy that I had taken on the job, moments like that made it all worthwhile.

Robert was basking in the glow of achievement, the cubs gathered around him full of hero worship. The moment of truth dawned, the kites soared upwards, flying beautifully then, as they climbed higher, one collapsed and began to fall from the sky, followed in quick succession by all the rest. The dowel rods were no good, they were too thin and couldn't stand the strain. Robert manfully admitted his mistake and offered to make new ones, but the moment of triumph had been lost and we retired to the church rooms where each cub was given a packet of jelly babies as consolation.

Some you win and some you lose. The kites might have been a disaster but spring was well on the way, the evenings were lengthening, and Scotland wood beckoned. Luckily Gorran is within easy walking distance to Scotland wood; the cubs loved the freedom – to be able to run and lay trails was their idea of heaven. By this time I had acquired another helper, a mum, Nona, who was a great sport and like me believed in getting the cubs into the great outdoors.

Scotland wood has a river running through it, ideal for Pooh sticks. This game proved to be a great success, until one over-enthusiastic cub got carried away and decided to go in the river, and under the bridge, to find out why his stick had not come out the other end. Rob, who was sometimes blackmailed into coming along, to get the fire going, was not impressed at having to wade in the river and hook out the adventurous cub.

'Wouldn't it be easier to just take them swimming, and have done with it?' he enquired.

'Too risky,' I replied, while wringing out a soggy cub jumper. 'At least they are working off some energy,' I continued.

'Pity we can't find a way of harnessing some of this energy, we could sell it to the national grid,' he answered as he grabbed out another small friend attempting to swim upstream.

When we had built all the fires, cooked the sausages, fallen in the stream and got stuck up the highest tree, then came the time to gather them all up and get them home. I suffered from recurring nightmares of arriving back at the church room minus a cub. I used to have visions of a frightened trembling little cub left behind in the wood, sheltering under a bush while darkness fell, waiting for us, to realise that we had left one behind.

Luckily it never happened, and I came to realise that my top priority was to get them all returned to their rightful owners; whether they were in mint condition or not was only of secondary importance. Just getting them back signified success.

All too soon the summer came to a close and the winter evenings began to draw in. By the second year, however, I was more in control of the situation, plus I had a helper. I worked on the philosophy of 'keep 'em busy, keep control' – let them loose and all hell breaks out. So we worked at gaining badges. One badge was learning to use a public telephone and we flogged it to death. Parents sitting quietly at home relishing an hour's respite from their offspring would thrill to the sound of a familiar piping voice yelling down the telephone.

'Mum?'

'Yes.'

'It's me.'

'Yes.'

'Jimmy.'

'Yes, hello.'

'Hello, Mum.'

'Hello, Jimmy.'

'Hello, Mum.'

'What are you doing?'

'Oh I'm learning to use the phone, in case of an emergency.'

'Well done.'

'Ewan's here too.'

'Good.'

'He wants to say hello.'

'Hello, Ewan, how are you?' silence at the other end of the phone, punctuated by giggles.

'Hello, anyone there?' more giggles then, 'Bye, Mum.'

I did feel by this stage that the least parents could do, as they were getting free babysitting, was participate in the proceedings in some small way, hence the phone calls. Occasionally I would feel really mean and let the pack loose on the village, 'bob-a-job' week, being an ideal time for this. The cubs would sally forth, complete with their cards to fill in and always full of enthusiasm.

'Do you want any jobs doing?' they would sweetly enquire of some naive householder.

'Well, you could tidy up the garden,' one sweet old lady replied, returning later to find that two very industrious cubs had neatly chopped off the heads of all her best geraniums.

Cars were washed by small hands, which lacked the motivation and strength to give any kind of finish, so many villagers drove around in smeary half-cleaned cars. Window washing was another favourite, which produced the same result. We all spent 'bob-a-job week' squinting through half-cleaned windows of some sort, or hastily re-planting our gardens.

But the thought was there, the cubs were learning to be useful, or so we had to believe, after all 'bob-a-job week' was a national institution, we were not meant to enjoy it, just survive it. Then, just when we thought it was all over, and we could settle down to some reasonably normal meetings, the brownies went up the church tower.

'Why can't we go up the tower like the brownies?' I was asked. 'It's not fair, we want to go.'

The cubs worked on the principle that if they kept on long enough, they would wear down my resistance, and they were right. The vicar at that time was a gentle mild-mannered man, who, because we held our meetings in the church rooms, felt it was his duty every so often to pay us a visit. Inevitably he seemed to choose the nights when the cubs were at their most exuberant. We would stand in the middle of the pack attempting to hold some kind of civilised conversation, while all hell was let loose around us. It was during one of these little visits that one of my older cubs broke away from the crowd and politely addressed the vicar.

'Do you think we could go up the church tower like the brownies?' he asked, with a sweet smile.

The vicar turned to me with a glazed look. 'How do you feel about this, Akela?' he asked.

'Well, I suppose if they all behave themselves,' I muttered weakly.

The vicar turned to the rest of the pack. 'What do you think, boys, would you like to go up the tower and have a tour of the church?'

The answer was deafening, 'yes please' they all bellowed.

There was no escape, it was on.

The appointed evening arrived. The vicar came to meet us at the church door, looking like a man going to the scaffold. He began by using delaying tactics, showing the pack around the church. Gorran church is a beautiful building, but I could see this was not what the cubs had in mind. They began to get restless, and it was obvious we could delay no longer, the moment had come.

We headed for the tower door, at the back of the church. The vicar had a torch, which only gave out a flickering light. He led the way, we followed. Some of the winding stone steps were crumbling. The light from the vicar's torch flickered in the distance, I was bringing up the rear, with Nona, my helper. Too late, I realised that a dark church tower, crumbling steps and twenty cubs do not make a good combination. My heart sank, as I realised that getting the pack up the tower and down again was going to prove quite a challenge.

We finally reached the top. The view was truly amazing, we could see right up to the white clay hills of St Austell, one way, and over to the Dodman and the sea, the other way. Gorran village, below us looked like toy town – it was breathtaking, for various reasons. The cubs were warned not to tread on the lead roof, but to walk around the edge. Also they were told not to lean over the edge to see what was going on down below.

'Cor look, that's my gran down there,' yelled Nicky, as he attempted to get a better view of his unsuspecting gran, who was quietly mowing her lawn.

'Gran, I'm up here, Gran!' he shouted, as he leant over the edge.

'Come back!' I shrieked, grabbing him by his green cub jumper, while trying to get hold of another intrepid adventurer who was attempting to continue the final ascent by going to the top-most pinnacle.

'Wonderful view,' observed the vicar calmly, gazing out over the Dodman.

'Yes, great,' I gulped, praying that we could start the downward ascent as soon as possible. It was one of those nightmare situations, where you promise yourself that if you get out of it unscathed, you will never tempt fate in such a way again.

CHAPTER ELEVEN
Surrounded by Sea

Because Cornwall has the sea on every side, except the bit which joins us to the rest of England, we all seem to form a close bond with water. So much so, that if we ever go to London, a mammoth trip to us Cornish, we always find ourselves making directly for the Thames and a boat trip. The same criteria applies to any city we find ourselves in, and has to be the result of living so close to the ocean.

'Let's get a boat,' I suggested to Rob, one hot sunny afternoon as we toiled up the long cliff path from Vault beach. The sight of other people happily chugging around to Vault, from Gorran Haven, had inspired me. I'd watched enviously as they landed faultlessly on the great curve of golden sand which is Vault beach. It seemed the ideal way of getting to those other secluded coves which are tucked away around the Cornish coast. Rob had always been keen on fishing, and having owned a boat in the past he didn't take much persuading. We looked around for a boat we could afford and finally found one at a boat sale. She was of Norwegian design, twelve feet long, clinker built, with a wide rounded middle and a curved Viking bow. Originally varnished, we spent ages rubbing her down and then painted her a deep royal blue. She sat in the water like a buoyant rubber duck. We added a Seagull engine and took to the high seas.

What I hadn't bargained for was the unbelievable change of character which happens to the male species when in charge of a boat. I have a theory that there is a dormant sea captain, lurking beneath the exterior of most men – put them in a boat and they become Captain Bligh in a jiffy. Rob assumed character every time he stepped aboard; the boat was of primary importance, the kids, the picnic and certainly the wife, all coming a poor second. My preconceived visions of gently landing at Vault beach went up in smoke The aim, upon landing, was I discovered to make sure that the boat did not come into contact with the beach – this could scrape the bottom, I was told. The result being that we were all made to abandon ship as soon as we were within swimming distance of the beach.

'Jump!' our intrepid captain would yell, and he was not averse to giving anyone chicken enough to linger on the edge of the boat, a helpful shove. We would stagger onto the beach, up to our necks in water if we were lucky, balancing the picnic, the bathers, and all other essential beaching equipment above our heads. In the early days, this would often include any tiny non-swimmers. Over the years this has naturally resulted in soggy picnics, wet towels, and children who have learnt to swim instantaneously.

Captain Bligh, however, having left us to our fate, would then proceed to moor up the boat, miles out from the beach. Once in position, he would spend at least fifteen minutes tying ropes, and checking that all was well, then he would dive over the side and swim for the shore carrying, obviously, nothing.

'Why can't we land like everyone else?' I would ask.

'The boat could get swamped, and the bottom scratched,' was the curt answer. I could see if I persisted I could well be keel-hauled for inciting a mutiny.

Vault beach is a mile-long curve of golden sand, situated between the Dodman and Penamaen Points. Landing on Vault is like arriving on some exotic island. Leaning over the side of the boat as you motor along, the sea is so clear you can look straight down through the azure depths to the sandy bottom. Sometimes you are lucky enough to catch a glimpse of the odd fish darting through the waving strands of seaweed. Sunday became our Vault day; I would make huge pasties, wrap them in tea towels, try and find a waterproof basket, grab all the bathers, and head for Portmellon. We always launched the boat at Portmellon, and then headed out across the bay, past Chapel Point and Gorran Haven, to Vault.

Christopher would meet friends from school and they would spend the day swimming and crabbing. The men would inevitably talk cricket, replaying every catch and moment of the previous day's game. The mums would just keep a watchful eye on the kids, while getting a good tan. None of us had ever heard of skin cancer, and the aim was to be the brownest body on the beach. One of our favourite pastimes – once we had sunbathed, gossiped and had enough swims – was to walk up to the other end of the beach, collecting shells and driftwood.

Then, gradually, we began to see the odd completely naked body, discreetly tucked up amongst the rocks. It was no big deal, they were at the very end of the beach, they were doing their thing, we were all happy. Then their numbers increased, obviously word got around, and they became more active – just lying down was not enough.

They indulged in all the usual beach games – cricket, rounders, swimming – bits and pieces would naturally bounce up and down during these activities, not only that, they began to spread down to our patch of beach. We all tried to ignore them, but remarks like, 'well he needn't have brought a cricket bat' or 'puts you right off your pasty, doesn't it?' definitely infiltrated our conversation.

I remember one Sunday afternoon, when the sun was so hot you could hardly bear to walk on the golden sand. A friend and I were strolling down to the water's edge to cool off, when a particularly well-endowed gentleman came strutting down the beach to where we stood. He was obviously extremely proud of his equipment, and intent on showing it off. He waded out past us, with a confident grin, and swam out in a small circle, surfacing again close to where we were paddling. My companion, a down-to-earth no-nonsense sort of lady, regarded our poser thoughtfully. As he emerged, directly in front of us, she took a deep breath, and said in a loud voice, 'Cor, what a difference the cold water makes, talk about a pimple on St Pauls.'

We both collapsed in giggles and our nudist, his ego deflated, as well as everything else, hurried past up the beach.

That was in the early days, when nudity was a rarity in Cornwall. Eventually there were so many bare bums we all got rather blasé about the whole thing, so much so, that some of the locals decided it was a case of 'if you can't beat them, join them'. I have to admit I always found this somewhat inhibiting to the natural flow of conversation, the squiggly bits acting as a kind of magnet to my eyes, regardless of the fact that my brain was telling me not to be so immature.

Beaches rose and waned in popularity. Vault was our Sunday beach but Great Perhaver, to the east of Gorran Haven, was a favourite as well. Accessible only by boat or a crumbling cliff path, it never got crowded, the most being only a few brave families who, like us, would arrive by boat. Great Perhaver had one distinctive characteristic – because of a huge ridge of sand halfway down the beach, waves are apt to appear from nowhere, even on a calm day. Arriving or leaving by boat, the last thing you want is the sudden, huge wave that appears, just as you are about to swing your leg over the side of the boat.

We were, of course, well trained by our experiences at Vault beach, and could leap over the side when landing, up to our necks in water, carrying the beach equipment and steadying the boat to prevent it going broadside to the waves. However, having spent an idyllic day on the beach there was always the knowledge, lurking at the back of your mind, we had to negotiate getting off again. This knowledge would generally be reinforced by the fact that we would be treated to the sight of some of the other boaters attempting to get their families and equipment off the beach without getting swamped. I've seen a calm sea suddenly produce a huge wave at that vital moment just before the engine starts, and endless boats going broadside, waves coming over the side, children screaming, and general mayhem. We would all rush down the beach to assist the victims, wading out chest-high in the water. Robert would always take command in these situations, issuing orders to the rest of us while slinging some unsuspecting visitor over his shoulder and placing her in the boat, which the rest of us would be holding steady. I think he secretly always fancied rescuing damsels in distress, and so the situation suited him down to the ground.

What did tend to rankle was the fact that I knew when it was our turn to launch, I would be the one left holding the boat steady while Rob attempted to start the engine. When the miracle finally happened, and the engine sprang into life, I was expected to perform a kind of pole vault, only without a pole, into the boat. This often resulted in me being hauled aboard like a stranded whale. No damsel in distress treatment for me. Whenever I see natives launching their canoes into a pounding surf, I think of Great Perhaver and our first little boat.

The seats on small boats are notoriously uncomfortable. I have found this out, the hard way, by accompanying Rob on various fishing trips over the years. I have a theory, that the reason so many men love fishing is the fact that they are reverting back to their caveman ancestors, the ones on whose hairy shoulders rested the responsibility of bringing back the dinosaur steak for dinner. The modern caveman will devote hundreds of hours to his role as 'man the hunter'. He will even have the gall to tell you how lucky you are to be getting free fish, when all the time you know that it would save you pounds to just pop into the fishmonger, rather than pay out for the boat, reels, rods etc.

To be fair, the one excellent plus side of all this is the fact that you know the fish is fresh, so fresh it's almost jumping on your plate. We have been through the whole fishing process, starting with a simple line to catch a mackerel, and progressing on to our own crab pots and finally, a net. The net, designed to catch crabs, only in fact caught spider crabs, so called because of their long, waving legs. Getting them out of the net was heartbreaking. 'Be careful of their legs,' I would implore Rob, never mind that they were destined for the pot, I always felt that they deserved a clean death rather than being pulled apart. My fisherman would grit his teeth, and over the years I realised that faint heart does not make a fisherwoman.

The final straw came one beautiful summer evening, when Rob had spent a very successful five hours out in the bay fishing. I had chickened out, and dutifully went to welcome my hunter home from the sea.

'Look at those,' he said proudly as he escorted me into the kitchen. I looked – there on the draining board were two huge fish. Their silver scales glistened in the late evening sun which was streaming in through the window. They were, truly, magnificent specimens – beautiful pollock, our favourite fish. I was duly impressed. I took a step forward, then gave a shriek – one of the fish was still breathing, great gasps came from its moving gills.

'It's still alive,' I uttered, 'we must put it back.'

'What?' Rob couldn't believe his ears. Without waiting for a reply, I grabbed a tea towel and wrapped the fish in it.

'I'm taking it back,' I said. It had put up such a fight for so long, it had to live. I made for the kitchen door, only to find my way barred.

What happened next, can only really be described as a tug of war, with the unfortunate fish as the rope. It was, without doubt, a battle of wills, I lost this particular battle – the fish ended up in the freezer where it stayed, uneaten, because I refused to cook it, and by that time nobody wanted to eat it. The situation has, I am happy to say, improved since those days. 'Put it back, Dad,' my daughter will shout when we are out fishing, and dad, twenty years on and well trained, will duly oblige. We now only keep fish which are shortly to peg out from old age.

CHAPTER TWELVE

Mevagissey Feast

Mevagissey Feast Week was something I had heard about since I was a child. My mother would often talk wistfully about feast week and chapel teas on the field. When she was growing up there were many chapels, all of which held their own celebrations for feast. 'How many chapels were there?' I would ask, and be amazed to hear her reel off a long list – Bible Christian, Wesleyan, Congregational, Methodist, and the Church, all competing to sing the best hymns, have the best teas. There were old photographs at home of long tables covered in white cloths, laden with saffron buns and cakes, and surrounded by ladies in white high-necked blouses with huge hats perched on their heads. Children in white starched pinafores sat at the tables, eager to get the photographs over and get down to the serious job of eating the tea.

Each chapel had its own day, and the quay would vibrate as the hymns were sung with gusto, startling the seagulls as they perched upon the harbour walls. Feast was the big date in the social calendar – everyone wore their best clothes, the men in suits with bowler hats, the streets packed with people, all intent on celebrating the feast of St Peter, the patron saint of Mevagissey.

Having heard so much about 'Feast', I had to experience it for myself. We lived on top of the hill, five minutes and we were in the middle of the town. Mevagissey was decorated with greenery, there was something on every night of the week. The male voice choir sang hymns on the quay in the setting sun, the brass band led the flora dance, the tune strangely captivating, the chords sounding so familiar as the band marched along.

They still had chapel teas, there was always an air of excitement hanging over the town. There was a fair over on the playing field, and a fete on the Saturday at the end of feast week, followed by a carnival. Rob, of course, was playing cricket on the Saturday, but a friend and her two children were coming over from Gorran to go to the carnival. We could hear the sound of the band drifting up over the hill.

Christopher and his friends were eager to go; we were just about to leave, when the dogs started barking and I realised that two bed-and-breakfast visitors were walking up the lane. Their timing couldn't have been worse. Generally I would always welcome visitors with a cup of tea and a chat; instead, I quickly whipped them upstairs, showed them the room, handed them a front door key, and left them to it.

We all ended up running down into Mevagissey to catch the carnival and then to go to the fair, and it was only when we were slowly making our way back up the hill that it dawned on me, that perhaps I had been taking rather a big chance, letting complete strangers into the house, giving them the key of the door and vanishing.

'What if everything has gone?' I said to Pat. She tried to reassure me, but I could see even she thought I had been a bit too hasty. I opened the front door with trepidation – after all, we had some nice bits of antique furniture which my family had given us – what if it was all gone?

Everything was fine, nothing had been touched. The visitors had gone out, leaving a note on the kitchen table, they would be back later. I breathed a sigh of relief, people were generally fine, I was pleased, it reinforced my inherent belief in human nature. I continued to hand out keys to all and sundry, and no one ever took advantage of it, perhaps it was the Cornish air.

Gorran, where we had lived when we first came to Cornwall, and where Christopher went to school, always had a church fete. Different than Mevagissey, because it was one event, it was nevertheless spoken of with a sense of occasion and everyone went. Gorran vicarage stood in its own grounds, which were large and which included a small lake surrounded by bamboo shoots and tiny winding paths. The first church fete I went to was like stepping back in time. Long trestle tables were covered with starched white cloths, cakes and cream teas were piled high, ladies with huge tea pots stood sentry, and we all sat on long benches in the hot, sheltered garden. Looking around me, I could see that all the mums had on their best dresses, the children were all polished and in pristine condition, all we needed were our hats to complete the scene. The vicarage was a graceful, black and white building, which looked more Italian than English, with a veranda upon which there would be various stalls. The band played in the evening, and there were sports and finally the flora dance, drifting out over the lawns. The scene was timeless, and I loved it. The children also loved it, but for a different reason – the lake with its long bamboos and winding paths was an adventurer's paradise. Once they had eaten their tea, they took off, disappearing into the bamboos, with shouts of joy.

'Be careful,' we told them, but the serenity of the place lulled us all into a sense of security. Occasionally a child would reappear, sometimes with wet feet, but nothing terrible ever happened and the sun always seemed to shine. Then the church decided that the old vicarage was not an economical proposition and so they sold it, and the church fete was never the same again. The setting and the atmosphere could never be recreated. I always felt lucky to have enjoyed a few of those old church fetes, I had a feeling that they were as near as I could get to the original church teas in the old photographs.

CHAPTER THIRTEEN

The Storm

Photograph by Sarah Vercoe

An easterly wind can suddenly whip up a previously sparkling blue sea into mountainous waves; this can happen within a few hours, and we have been caught on the beach, attempting to launch the boat, having to dice with death to get off the beach and back to the safety of the harbour.

One of the worse storms I remember began softly, a light breeze on the early morning air, which gathered momentum as the day wore on. Christopher went to school at Gorran, just over the hill from Church Park, and this meant driving through Portmellon which sat right on the water's edge. One row of cottages sit facing straight out to sea, the water lapping at their edge, with only the road in between them and the sea. The other cottages are cannily clinging to the cliff at the side of the cove, and so avoid taking the full force of the waves. Rob's father remembered when there was no road across the top of the beach, just a shingle track.

When an easterly storm was blowing, the waves would pound into the sea wall, hit it, and be thrown up onto the road, drenching any driver foolish enough to attempt to get across. Very often the might of the sea would produce enormous waves which would be flung higher than the cottages and would then crash down over the roofs.

When I first moved to Cornwall, dodging the waves during an easterly storm became quite a challenge – timing was the key, you waited until you spied a lull, when the sea was taking a breather, you accelerated and sped through the foaming water, coming out the other side the victor.

Rob was full of advice, 'Wait for the third wave, and never attempt it when the waves are breaking over the roofs of the cottages.' He would recount the story of a guy who attempted to beat the waves and whose car stalled, leaving him to crawl out along the road, lucky to be alive, while his car was washed into the sea and reduced to a pile of metal when the tide went out.

When the water was wild, people would gather at either side of the cove to watch the waves and an added attraction was to see who would be foolhardy enough to attempt to run the gauntlet of the waves. Innocent summer visitors were always good sports, they would often leave their car windows down, and arrive at the other side, awash. I remember seeing an old Austin Seven approaching from the Gorran side, he didn't even slow down.

'He's never coming across!' I gasped. He gave a cocky wave of his arm to the watching crowd and accelerated across. His timing wasn't good – a huge wave hit the road, the old car was enveloped in water. I closed my eyes, expecting the worse. When I opened them he came steaming on; the driver, no longer waving and distinctly bedraggled, headed up the hill towards Mevagissey. How he did it I'll never know.

My own cavalier attitude to the waves came one morning while doing the school run. I had Christopher and a friend in the back and was full of confidence in my ability to get the timing right. The sea does not appreciate confidence, and halfway across decided to send a huge wave catching us exactly midway. The car stalled, and I began to panic – I knew that another wave could begin to draw the car towards the sea. Luckily the men at the boatyard had seen what had happened and they shouted at us to stay in the car, while they waited for the required lull and pushed us to the safety of the boatyard. The kids were silent in the back; like me, they had been scared at the unrelenting power of the sea.

Rob came along with the tractor shortly afterwards and he loaded the kids up into the transport box, usually used for sheep, and they were carried to school in style, with a great playground story of waves smashing the car, and minutes to live, to impress their friends.

So when another storm began to brew I was ready to batten down the hatches. It threatened all day and by early evening the thorn trees lining our lane were bent double as the wind howled its way up towards the old cob walls, hammering at the stable front door and screaming around the windows.

Rob arrived back from the farm on foot.

'I've had to leave the tractor at the boat yard,' he informed me, 'can't get across.'

'Some storm,' I said.

'I've known worse,' was Rob's reply. He is convinced that he has known worse, and always will; whatever happens he has the countryman's superiority, having seen wilder, colder, more extreme weather than anyone ever. I found this attitude slightly annoying because it always managed to take the wind out of my sails, but this was all about to change.

The storm raged. Rob went out to the wood pile to stock up the fire and came back looking as though he had been in a hurricane. The dogs huddled together, and when we finally went to bed it felt as though we were right in the middle of it, being on top of the hill we were getting the full force of the gale.

Sometime in the early hours there was an almighty crash. Rob struggled into his clothes to investigate and discovered two of the trees, which grew along the edge, had been blown down.

'Nothing I can do now,' he said, 'have to wait until morning.'

With the arrival of daylight, we were greeted by a sight of devastation – the lane was completely blocked. There was no way we could get the car out. Rob set off to walk to Bodrugan and Christopher and I decided to go with him as far as Portmellon to see the waves. We began to realise that this had not been just any old storm.

We decided to walk down to Portmellon to see how the cove had fared. I will never forget the sight that greeted us, the sea had completely washed away a huge chunk of the road beside the Rising Sun pub, leaving a gaping hole. We edged our way past the pub and gazed across towards the line of cottages which faced the sea. The end cottage had taken the worst of the sea. The sea wall had been flattened by the force of the waves and great pieces of stone had been hurled high into the air smashing the wooden storm shutters, breaking the glass and allowing the waves to rush in through the windows, flattening the walls and running out at the back of the house and up the valley. Where there had been windows, there were only great gaping holes. Luckily no one had been hurt; when the waters began to seep through the wooden shutters, the occupants had realised that they had to get out.

Even old 'I've seen worse', was speechless. Some of the boats which had been parked in the boatyard were picked up and ended two fields up the valley. The scene was one of utter devastation. Rob ended up helping to salvage some bits and pieces from 'Sandy Cove', the cottage on the end which had taken the hardest pounding. In Mevagissey a row of new houses which had just been completed behind the museum were simply demolished, washed away, nobody had had the chance to move into them, which in hindsight was a good thing.

Such is the force of the sea, unrelenting and unpredictable, you have to respect its power.

That was, without doubt, the worst storm in my memory, and even Rob had to agree that it was unique. The sea still pounds in at Portmellon, the waves still break over the houses, the roof of 'Rock Cottage' opposite the pub still gets stone damage most winters, and we still have to check the state of the tide if there's an easterly blowing. Come the summer there will always be visitors who cannot get their heads around the fact that the waves smash onto the road – so wave, watching beside the pub with a pint in your hand – it still provides much better entertainment than any television.

CHAPTER FOURTEEN

Two For The Price of One?

When I found out that I was pregnant, I made two decisions. The first was that I saw no need to go through all the prodding and endless examinations, spending hours in waiting rooms, that I had gone through when I was expecting Christopher in Plymouth. This time, knowing more about the whole birth process, I would call the shots. Also, I planned to have a little girl, thus completing our family nicely. The plan was set, little did I know, the best laid plans etc., etc…

I did visit the local doctor once, to confirm that I was actually pregnant, and having got that over I got on with my life. We had planned a holiday in September, 'can't go away in the summer, because of the farm,' Rob always said, adding casually, 'and the cricket.'

Talking to other cricket wives, I was surprised to learn that none of the cricketers actually left the parish in the cricket season. None of them got married in the cricket season, and looking around I learnt that most babies were born during the winter months if at all possible; wives who gave birth during the hallowed time were regarded as irresponsible. Marriages were not encouraged on Saturdays during the season, you had to fit them in at the beginning or at the end.

Our holiday, after a summer of cubs, beach, visitors, and most important cricket, was to be on a cruiser on the Thames. This idea had appealed to us both, due obviously to the fact that we would be: a) in a boat, and b) on water for the entire holiday.

We decided to take Bambi, our younger dog, but to leave Bess behind to be looked after back at the farm. She would be able to lie in the sun, and give advice to Panda, the new Bodrugan dog.

We set off in high spirits, Christopher and Bambi, in the back. The boatyard was at Hampton Court, which we found after driving around for ages, falling out over my idea of directions, and generally wishing we had stayed in Cornwall. However, once we all sighted water and boats, happiness took over, and we piled aboard for our instruction from the boat owner. Rob told him immediately that we had our own boat at home, and so the instructions were kept to the minimum. He omitted to say that our boat was only twelve feet long on a good day. We dropped the boat owner off and headed upstream.

I began stowing away our provisions and started to explore the cruiser. This didn't actually take that long, and I had to retrace my steps, because I had some how missed our bedroom. There were two bunks in the bow, for Christopher and Bambi, but where were we going to sleep?

'I thought this was a four-berth boat,' I yelled to Rob, who was up top at the tiller.

'It is,' he replied.

'Well I can't see where we are going to sleep,' I said.

'Take the tiller,' he instructed, and disappeared below. He returned in minutes, 'on the table,' he said, laughing. 'It folds down, great isn't it?'

It was great, the scenery was wonderful, we were 'up country' but on water. The boat wasn't exactly what I had had in mind when I booked it – 'basic' should have definitely been the buzz word in the brochure, but what the hell, we chugged merrily upstream.

Then we approached our first lock; other boats were lining up, waiting to go in. 'Get on the bow, ready to jump onto that pontoon,' Rob yelled.

I stared at him, in amazement, it was like being at home, Captain Bligh had resurfaced with a vengeance, and this time it wasn't a beach that we were landing on, it was a very narrow strip of wood which, if I missed, meant I would go straight into the water. There was not time to argue, Christopher was given the stern rope, we headed for the pontoon. I jumped and clung to a wooden support for dear life.

'Hang on,' Rob yelled, 'tie her up.'

I did as I was told. I knew, looking at his face, that male pride was in command, he didn't want to look a fool in front of all the other boats – we were from Cornwall, we knew what we were doing.

The lock filled, and it was our turn to edge our way in. We managed to do this without mishap, then, when everything was going well, the dog, eager to see what was going on, fell into the lock. All our seamanship went to the wall.

'Bambi's in the lock.'

'Get the boat hook.'

'She will drown, get her out, get her out.'

Panic took over, Rob yelled, Christopher hung perilously over the stern, attempting to grab Bambi who gamely kept swimming around in circles until, finally, Rob grabbed her out.

Bambi shivered violently, but after I had wrapped her in a towel and cuddled her, she began to feel better, but spent the rest of the holiday peeping over the side, waiting for us to moor up before she could run on the bank. I noticed she was very careful when we did stop for her to go ashore, sizing up the distance from boat to bank with great precision. We had called her Bambi because she was a cross between a whippet and something else long vanished into the distance of time. She had a black, sleek, short-haired coat, and the most expressive eyes. She loved Bess and Church Park, but she adapted to life on the boat very well, after her first mishap.

Once out of the lock, we motored upstream, gobsmacked at the luxurious houses which lined the banks of the Thames. Each one had its dinghy parked at the bottom of the garden, the dinghy being a huge motor launch – we were well impressed. The plan was to make our way to Windsor, where we would meet up with my cousins from Harrow who were going to join us for a day cruising on the river. Their son was a bit younger than Christopher, and they got on really well. We spent the night at Windsor and the family duly arrived the following morning. We set sail, upstream.

While making our way to Windsor, we had realised that the toilet facilities required forethought – you had to think before you performed, and to go ashore for anything of major importance. Thus when John and Sheila arrived, our first suggestion was, 'if you want to do anything more than a wee, do it now, before we set off.'

They assured us that they were under control in that area, and we set off. The sun was shining, the trees along the bank, beginning to turn a wonderful golden colour, we negotiated the first lock, near Windsor and chugged upstream. A bottle of wine was produced and we were enjoying the good life when the first drama struck.

'Where's Christopher?' his younger cousin suddenly appeared, looking puzzled.

'Down below,' I answered, taking another swig, while waving to another boatload of Sunday cruisers.

Two minutes later, he reappeared, 'He's not down there,' he said, looking worried.

We all stopped talking and I made for the hatchway at record speed. Because the boat was so small, there was only the saloon, loo and Christopher's bedroom in the bow – I covered the distance in two minutes flat. There was no sign of him, panic immediately set in. We had started off making him wear a life jacket, but because it was big and clumsy, and because he could swim, this had been abandoned. Now he had obviously fallen over, probably way back, and because we had been drinking wine and chatting, no one had noticed. The two boys had been together, or so we'd assumed.

I dashed up top, 'He's not there!' I yelled, 'he's fallen over, turn round.'

Rob left the tiller and, like me, did a two-minute search of the boat, then just as I was about to have a seizure, he noticed a guilty look in young Robert's eye. 'Where is he?' he roared, and we were led to a small cupboard in the saloon, Rob opened the door, and there he was.

'It was a joke,' both boys protested.

'A joke which nearly gave your mother a heart attack,' Rob answered.

The rest of the day was happily uneventful; the boys, realising that they had overstepped the mark, settled down, and my blood pressure subsided. Then we had to turn around and motor back down to Windsor. By now the sun had vanished behind some nasty-looking clouds, but we had had a great day, and tied up for a meal before disembarking our passengers. Then we made our way towards the last lock of the day, and were surprised to see no sign of life on the bank. Where was the lock keeper?

The rain was coming down, quite steadily now, and dusk was falling; we could see the lights of Windsor in the distance, but couldn't actually get there. Robert and John scrambled up the bank to read a small notice on the side of the lock, which informed boaters that after six o'clock the lock was not manned and had to be worked manually. This resulted in the two men sweating at the lock handles, rain pouring down, the rest of us giggling from the comfort of the boat.

The next day, we were off again, and there was mutiny on board. We travelled upstream, passing through quite a few locks, and each time the tying up became more scary, the jumping to the pontoon more erratic. Finally, at one lock, I had such a close shave, jumping and nearly missing, left hanging onto the bollard for dear life, while having lost the mooring rope completely. The captain, red-faced and indignant at my lack of agility, was surprised to find that I had gone on strike.

'That's it,' I said, 'I'm doing the driving, you can ****** well jump.'

Having got that sorted, the holiday proceeded without any more dramas.

Christmas was coming closer, the cubs made Christmas cards, and went around Gorran singing carols, in high warbley voices, punctuated by frequent fits of the giggles. The school carol service at Gorran church was a tradition, as was the Christmas play, parents always supported these events, strongly, and because it was a small community everyone knew the children performing, having watched most of them grow up. Comments like, 'he sounds just like his father' or 'boy Bunney's grown up, can't sing though' would filter through the congregation.

Christmas Eve was always celebrated at The Barley Sheaf' in Gorran, the place was always packed, a sense of excitement hung over the old stone pub, and many of the revellers would trundle across to the church later for the midnight service. Mothers would be discussing the next day's turkey, cooking hints being swopped with gay abandon, everyone having the perfect way to cook the turkey and then, as the evening wore on, the disaster stories would emerge – the turkey which wouldn't fit into the oven; the one which took for ever to cook; the one which slipped out of the pan, and landed on the floor, skidding over, straight into the waiting mouth of the amazed dog.

Much laughter and merriment would continue, until the time to depart came, and everyone came out into the crisp night air and made their way back to fill Christmas sacks and stuff turkeys, until finally falling into bed, only to be woken three hours later, by the immortal words, 'Father Christmas has been, guess what he's brought me?'

I always found this the hardest thing to bear, having just packed it all, then hearing dear old Father Christmas getting all the credit.

January dawned, bringing rain, and the dogs would wander out for a few minutes, see the weather and beat a hasty retreat back to their beds. I, meanwhile, was steadily getting larger and larger. I could balance a cup and saucer on my stomach, and mobility was becoming quite a problem. Basically I felt like a baby elephant, but I carried on regardless.

I did have an appointment with the doctor, Bill Hannan, who gave me the once-over, and booked me in for an appointment at the anti-natal clinic in Penrice Hospital at St Austell. Bill Hannan was a very sociable man, and we chatted about various things while he was completing his examination.

'I do seem to be very large,' I said, 'you don't think it could be twins do you?'

Bill laughed, and said 'no', and that was that. Penrice hospital duly examined me, and said all was well, so I continued to balance my cup and saucer, plus a plate, on the bump, and carried on regardless.

The cubs had entered an indoor football league, and one Saturday in February we spent the afternoon at the local sports centre in providing transport, and support to our pack. It was a long afternoon and I was pleased to get home and put my feet up; the baby was due within three weeks. At about nine thirty that evening I got up to make a cup of coffee and realised something was happening.

'I think we ought to go to the hospital,' I said, and Rob, who had been dozing in the chair, leapt up immediately. We piled into our Mini and made our way to St Austell. There was no panic, I was just pleased that things were getting going.

Arriving at Penrice, I was astounded to be told that I had to go to Truro because the baby was early. This took me completely by surprise – it was at least half an hour into Truro, and by now it was getting late. I felt that they were being picky. However, I toddled back out to the Mini, and Christopher waiting expectantly, and started for Truro.

The sense of calm had, by now, begun to evaporate. I was getting quite strong pains now, and the thought of trundling to Truro at that time of night was a bit worrying. Rob was seriously concentrating on his driving, and I tried not to time the contractions. I kept thinking about stories I had read in the papers about babies being born in the back of cars. I glanced back into the Mini, it would certainly be cramped, then I tried to think of something good, and realised Rob was used to delivering lambs on the farm. Well, I thought, he'll have a good idea of what to do if the situation arises. Having consoled myself with this thought, I settled down to the drive.

We pulled into Treliske Hospital, and all heaved a sigh of relief. The nursing staff took over. Rob faintly offered to stay but I knew how squeamish he was – one drop of blood and he would faint. Lambing, he could manage, if it was straight forward; a cow calving was another thing altogether – any caesarean, and he always had to beat a hasty retreat out of the calving shed.

So I was left to it, and everything began to happen with amazing speed. This is great, I thought, I'll get it all over and then get some sleep. The nurse introduced a young midwife, 'You will be her first delivery,' she said. I attempted to smile between contractions, but I was concentrating.

'Everything's fine,' she said, 'when you are ready.'

I was ready, the baby, was born. 'He's very small, I heard them say, then, 'he needs to go to special care.'

I was tired, and due to inhaling enormous amounts of gas and air, was on a high. Then the little midwife leaned over me, she was saying something which didn't make sense, 'There's another, Mrs Bunney.'

'Another what?'

'Another baby.'

The words slowly penetrated my fuddled mind. The woman was mad. I pulled myself up to gaze down at my stomach, I couldn't believe what I saw – half of the enormous bump had gone, the other half was still round.

'We are going to have to cut her,' I heard. That did it. I raised myself up. 'Don't you dare to cut me!' I bellowed.

My little midwife looked scared. I was reckoning on common sense – by this stage, the law of averages, if one baby came out, the next one, or ones could follow. My mind was in a whirl, I had a sudden vision of a magician pulling rabbits out of a hat, with me being the hat.

The second baby was born. 'Any more?' I asked.

'No that's it,' they said.

'Thank God for that,' I sighed.

'Well aren't you lucky, Mrs Bunney, one of each – two for the price of one.'

76

The words 'two for the price of one' whirled around my head – was I dreaming? Was it real? Would I wake up soon? I gingerly slid my hand down to the famous bump – it had gone, it was for real. Rob had gone home with Christopher, to Church Park, to await one baby – how would he feel when he found out that there were two babies? I lay in the recovery room, frantically trying to understand and come to terms with the situation. Two babies meant two prams, two of everything; we had planned for only one – how would we cope?

Rob, meanwhile, had spent a peaceful night, but waking early had rushed down to Portmellon to use the phone box and find out whether it was a boy or a girl. The nurse at the other end began with the words, 'We have a surprise for you, your wife has had twins – a boy and a girl – congratulations!'

This totally unexpected news rendered Rob speechless, and all he could do to Christopher, who was with him, was put up two fingers – words for once in his life having completely failed him.

Finally the penny dropped and he rushed around to all our friends babbling about two, and still holding up two fingers.

Down at Treliske on a bright sunny Cornish February morning I began to plan the future. The babies were going to be fine. I realized that these two would be proper Cornish, lucky enough to be born in one of the most beautiful counties. We didn't have much money, but we had the most important things in life – we certainly had more than enough love for these two unexpected babies and we had the beach. What more could anyone want? We were rich indeed.